"CALL ON ME"

Powerful Supplications
for Healing, Protection
&
Fulfillment of Needs

By
Shaykh Hisham Kabbani

Institute for Spiritual & Cultural Advancement

Library of Congress Cataloging-in-Publication Data

TBD

Published and Distributed by:
Institute for Spiritual and Cultural Advancement
17195 Silver Parkway, #401
Fenton, MI 48430 USA
Tel: (888) 278-6624
Fax:(810) 815-0518
Email: info@sufilive.com
Web: http://www.sufilive.com
First Edition May 2019
ISBN: 978-1-938058-51-6

Printed in the United States of America.

Contents

Dedication vi
About the Author vii
Transliteration Notes x
Introduction 1
The Best Times to Make *Duʿā* 7
The Etiquette of Asking Allah 9
Supplications Containing Allah's Greatest Name 21
1) Two Verses in the Holy Qur'an 22
2) *Duʿā* of Sayyīdinā Yūnus and to Die as a Martyr 23
3) *Sahābah*'s *Duʿā* for Specific Needs 25
Hadith of ʿAbdullāh Ibn Buraydah 25
Hadith of Anas ibn Mālik 26
4) Overcoming Tribulation 28
Raising One's Head Skywards 28
Hadith of Anas 29
Supplications for Calamities 30
Prevention of Affliction 31
When Afflicted with Calamity 32
Hadith of the Thief 32
Salvation from Punishment 35
Ease from the Trumpet-Blast 35
Sultan al-Awlīyā's Prescription for Overall Protection 38
Duʿā of Need 39

بسم الله الرحمن الرحيم

In the Name of Allah, the Compassionate, the Merciful

ادعوني أستجب لكم

"Call on Me, I will Respond to You All."

Sūrah Ghāfir (The Forgiver) 40:60

DEDICATION

It is my immense honor to dedicate this book to the love of Prophet Muḥammad ﷺ, and to all the people of *Ahlu 's-Sunnah wa 'l-Jama'ah* whose hearts beat with the mention of Sayyīdinā Muḥammad ﷺ and his *Ṣaḥāba* ؓ with the deepest respect, and who affirm that their supplications are answered by the honor of Sayyīdinā Muḥammad ﷺ, who is the intercessor of all prayers before Allah the Exalted.

This book is also dedicated to the *shuyūkh* of the eminent Golden Chain of the Naqshbandi Sufi Order, especially to Sayyīdī Shaykh Muḥammad Nāẓim 'Adil al-Ḥaqqānī ق and all his followers, and similarly, to all *mashaykh* of other esteemed *ṭarīqats* and their followers.

May Allāh ﷻ grant them a share in the rewards of this humble effort.

Shaykh Muḥammad Hisham Kabbani
May 2019/Ramadan 1440

ABOUT THE AUTHOR

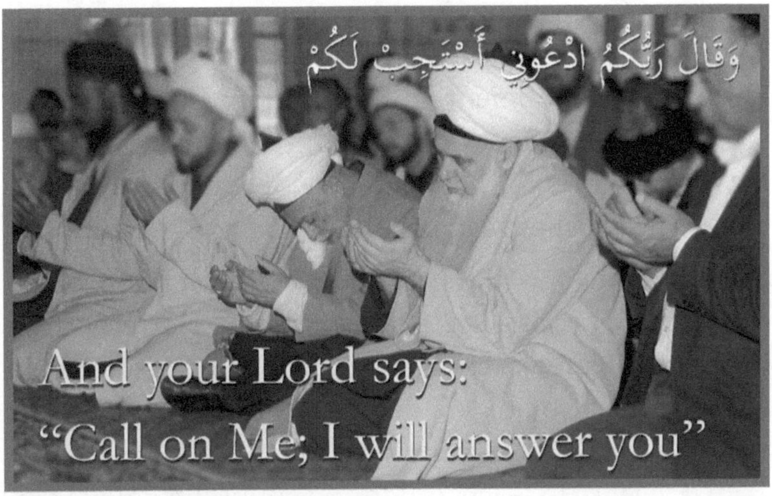

Shaykh Hisham Kabbani, with his master, Mawlana Shaykh Nazim al-Haqqani in Uzbekistan, 2001, as part of a global tour.

Shaykh Muḥammad Hisham Kabbani is a world-renowned religious scholar and author. He has devoted his life to the promotion of the traditional Islamic principles of peace, tolerance, love, compassion and brotherhood, while opposing extremism in all its forms. The shaykh is a member of a respected family of traditional Islamic scholars, which includes the former head of the

Association of Muslim Scholars of Lebanon and the present Grand Mufti[1] of Lebanon.

In the U.S., Shaykh Kabbani serves as Chairman, Islamic Supreme Council of America; Founder, Naqshbandi Sufi Order of America; Advisor, World Organization for Resource Development and Education; Chairman, As-Sunnah Foundation of America; Chairman, Kamilat Muslim Women's Organization; and, Founder and President, The Muslim Magazine.

Shaykh Kabbani is highly trained, both as a Western scientist and as a classical Islamic scholar. He received a bachelor's degree in chemistry and studied medicine. In addition, he also holds a degree in Islamic Divine Law, and under the tutelage of Shaykh 'Abd Allah Daghestani ق, license to teach, guide and counsel religious students in Islamic spirituality from Shaykh Muḥammad Nazim Adil al-Qubrusi al-Haqqani an-Naqshbandi ق, the world leader of the Naqshbandi-Haqqani Sufi Order.

His books include: *Hierarchy of Saints* (2016), *The Fiqh of Islam* (2014),*The Peacemakers* (2012), *Jihad: Principles of Leadership in War and Peace* (2010), *Banquet for the Soul (2008), A Spiritual Commentary on the Chapter of Sincerity (2006), Sufi Science of Self-Realization* (Fons Vitae, 2005), *Keys to the Divine Kingdom* (2005); *Classical Islam and the Naqshbandi Sufi Order* (2004); *The Naqshbandi Sufi*

[1] The highest Islamic religious authority in the country.

Tradition Guidebook (2004); *The Approach of Armageddon? An Islamic Perspective* (2003); *Encyclopedia of Muḥammad's Women Companions and the Traditions They Related* (1998, with Dr. Laleh Bakhtiar); *Encyclopedia of Islamic Doctrine* (7 vols. 1998); *Angels Unveiled* (1996); *The Naqshbandi Sufi Way* (1995); *Remembrance of God Liturgy of the Sufi Naqshbandi Masters* (1994).

In his long-standing endeavor to promote better understanding of classical Islam, Shaykh Kabbani has hosted two international conferences in the United States, both of which drew scholars from throughout the Muslim world. As a resounding voice for traditional Islam, his counsel is sought by journalists, academics and government leaders.

TRANSLITERATION NOTES

The following symbols are universally recognized and have been respectfully included in this work:

The symbol ﷺ represents *ṣall-Allahu ʿalayhi wa sallam* (Allah's blessings and greetings of peace be upon him), which is customarily recited after reading or pronouncing the holy name of Prophet Muḥammad ﷺ.

The symbol ؑ represents *ʿalayhi 's-salām* (peace be upon him/her), which is customarily recited after reading or pronouncing the holy names of the other prophets, family members of Prophet Muḥammad ﷺ, the pure and virtuous women in Islam, and the angels.

The symbol ؓ/ؓ represents *raḍī-Allahu ʿanhu/ʿanhā* (may Allah be pleased with him/her), which is customarily recited after reading or pronouncing the holy names of Companions of the Prophet ﷺ.

INTRODUCTION

Our weapon is not a sword or a knife, a gun or a stone, our weapon is *du'ā*!

عَنْ عَلِيٍّ رَضِيَ اللهُ عَنْهُمْ قَالَ : قَالَ رَسُولُ اللهِ ﷺ : " الدُّعَاءُ سِلَاحُ الْمُؤْمِنِ ، وَعِمَادُ الدِّينِ ، وَنُورُ السَّمَاوَاتِ وَالْأَرْضِ"

The Prophet ﷺ said:

> The *du'ā* is the weapon of the believer, the pillar of the religion and the Light of Heavens and Earth.[1]

Du'ā can take away every problem and it can give you the Light of Heavens and Earth! It can be used as a weapon against Shaytan for what he does against your soul, it will remove your bad desires and it will be a weapon against illness and a pillar supporting your religion.

Allah ﷻ erases and confirms whatever He wants and the only thing that can erase what is written for you is the *du'ā*.

---

[1] *Mustadrak* al-Ḥākim from 'Alī ؓ.

عَنْ ثَوْبَانَ وَفِي رِوَايَتِهِمَا : لَا يَرُدُّ الْقَدَرَ إِلَّا الدُّعَاءُ وَلَا يَزِيدُ فِي الْعُمُرِ
إِلَّا الْبِرُّ ، وَإِنَّ الرَّجُلَ لَيُحْرَمُ الرِّزْقَ بِالذَّنْبِ يُذْنِبُهُ

Thawbān ﵁ related:

> Nothing will repel Destiny except the *duʿā* and nothing increases the lifespan except goodness, and indeed a man is prevented from his provision by a sin he commits.[2]

If, for example, it is written that you will go out of this door and fall and break your leg, *duʿā* will prevent it. So if you are aware of this and you begin everything you do with *duʿā*—when you stand for prayer, upon entering a mosque, upon leaving your house, or when you wake up or sleep, or begin to speak with someone, etc.—and you begin by reciting *"Bismillāhi 'r-Raḥmāni 'r-Raḥīm"* or *al-Fātiḥa* or another *duʿā*, then with the *barakah* of the *duʿā* Allah will erase the difficulty that was written for you that you are not seeing. That is why we should always be asking Allah ﷻ through *duʿā* and that is the importance of *duʿā*: it brings healing and takes affliction from you!

---

[2] Āḥmad, ibn Mājah and Tirmidhī.

عَنْ أَبِي سَعِيدٍ الْخُدْرِيِّ قَالَ : سَمِعْتُ رَسُولَ اللَّهِ ﷺ يَقُولُ : مَنْ رَأَى مِنْكُمْ مُنْكَرًا فَلْيُغَيِّرْهُ بِيَدِهِ ، فَإِنْ لَمْ يَسْتَطِعْ فَبِلِسَانِهِ ، فَإِنْ لَمْ يَسْتَطِعْ فَبِقَلْبِهِ ، وَذَلِكَ أَضْعَفُ الْإِيمَانِ .

The Prophet ﷺ said:

> Whoever sees something wrong should try to change it with his hand and if he cannot, then with his tongue and if he cannot, then with his heart and that is the weakest level of faith.[3]

Changing "by hand" would be to write to someone (such as an apology) and try to change a wrong you committed. If you cannot, then change it with your tongue by speaking and if not with your tongue, then by your heart through *duʿā,* and that is the weakest of *imān,* faith. Without making *duʿā,* you will not be safe and your illnesses will not be cured, especially spiritual illnesses.

عَنْ أَبِي سَعِيدٍ رضي الله عنه أَنَّ النَّبِيَّ ﷺ قَالَ : "مَا مِنْ مُسْلِمٍ يَدْعُو بِدَعْوَةٍ لَيْسَ فِيهَا إِثْمٌ وَلَا قَطِيعَةُ رَحِمٍ إِلَّا أَعْطَاهُ اللَّهُ بِهَا إِحْدَى ثَلَاثٍ : إِمَّا أَنْ تُعَجَّلَ لَهُ دَعْوَتُهُ ، وَإِمَّا أَنْ يَدَّخِرَهَا لَهُ فِي الْآخِرَةِ ، وَإِمَّا أَنْ يَصْرِفَ عَنْهُ مِنَ السُّوءِ مِثْلَهَا ، قَالُوا : إِذًا نُكْثِرُ ؟ قَالَ : اللَّهُ أَكْثَرُ ".

---

[3] Muslim.

The Prophet ﷺ said:

> There is no Muslim who calls upon Allah with words in which there is no sin or cutting of family ties except Allah will give him one of three things: either He will answer his prayer soon, or He will store it up for him in the Hereafter, or He will remove something bad from him that is equivalent to what he is asking for.
>
> They said, "Then we should make a great amount of *du'ā*."
>
> He said, "Allah is greater."[4]

عَنْ عَائِشَةَ -رَضِيَ اللّٰهُ عَنْهَا- قَالَتْ: قَالَ رَسُولُ اللّٰهِ ﷺ: إِنَّ اللّٰهَ يُحِبُّ الْمُلِحِّينَ فِي الدُّعَاءِ.

Sayyida 'Āishā ؓ related that the Prophet ﷺ said:

> Truly Allah likes the one who keeps insisting (pestering) with the *du'ā*.[5]

Keep asking, "*Yā Rabb, Yā Rabb* (help me)!" as Allah likes that. Keep bugging (pestering)! "Insisting" is not the right word; Prophet ﷺ said "*al-mulīḥīn*" is the one who overdoes it, so bug Paradise, bug the angels! "*Allāh, Yā Allāh, Yā Allāh, Yā Allāh*!" then Allah will say, "*Yā 'abdī*, O My servant!" The Prophet ﷺ said that Allah likes the one who is always bugging, insisting, overdoing in

[4] Tirmidhī.

[5] al-Awza'ī.

asking Him. Therefore, O Muslims, O believers, O *mu'min*! Keep bugging, keep asking and keep praying and making *du'ās* and you will be cured from many physical and spiritual sicknesses that you know or don't even perceive. May Allah open our eyes and our minds so we will always be on the right way!

عَنْ أَنَسٍ عَنِ النَّبِيِّ ﷺ: لَا تَعْجِزُوا فِي الدُّعَاءِ فَإِنَّهُ لَا يَهْلِكُ مَعَ الدُّعَاءِ أَحَدٌ.

Anas related that the Prophet ﷺ said:

> Don't be lazy with *du'ā* for no one will be destroyed due to making *du'ā*.[6]

Sayyīdinā Mūsā was asking Allah for forty years to free Banī Isrā'īl from Pharoah and his tyranny. When Sayyīdinā Mūsā asked Allah, "When are you going to destroy Pharoah for me?" Allah said, "Tomorrow." He said, "How tomorrow?" Then Allah said:

أَلَيْسَ الصُّبْحُ بِقَرِيبٍ

alaysa 'ṣ-ṣubḥu bi qarīb

"*Is not the morning nigh?*" (Surat Hūd, 11:81)

Allah ﷻ spoke to him directly, "Don't push, I am going to destroy him."

Sayyīdinā Mūsā said, "I didn't see anything."

---

[6] Ḥākim's *al-Mustadrak*.

"No, you will see everything," Allah replied, and Allah showed Sayyīdinā Mūsā ﷺ how to destroy Pharoah.

Allah said to Mūsā ﷺ, "You are the highest. You don't need to destroy them with a cane, I will destroy them by drowning them in the ocean so they don't appear again."

This means "Don't lose hope with *duʿā* by saying, 'I made *duʿā* but it didn't work, so I will stop.'" No, don't stop! Rather remember the hadith:

قَالَ أَنَسٍ : قَالَ رَسُولُ اللهِ ﷺ: لَا يَزَالُ الْعَبْدُ بِخَيْرٍ مَا لَمْ يَسْتَعْجِلْ ، قَالُوا : يَا رَسُولَ اللهِ كَيْفَ يَسْتَعْجِلُ ؟ قَالَ : يَقُولُ قَدْ دَعَوْتُ رَبِّي فَلَمْ يَسْتَجِبْ لِي.

The Prophet ﷺ said:

> The servant is always in a good way as long as he does not rush.
>
> They asked: "O Prophet of Allah, how does he rush?"
>
> He ﷺ said, "He says, 'I prayed to my Lord and He did not respond to me.'"[7]

When you rush you don't get anything! Allah will not grant your request and then you say, "I asked and my *duʿā* was not accepted."

[7] related by Sayyīdinā Anas ﷺ in Āḥmad's *Musnad*.

1

افضل اوقات لالدعاء

THE BEST TIMES TO MAKE *DUʿĀ*

There are six times in which *duʿā* is most accepted:

1) ***Ath-thuluth al-akhīr min al-layl.*** The last third of the night before *Ṣalāt al-Fajr* by two hours, which is the time of *qiyām* when everyone is sleeping. At that time you can focus well and meditate on what you are asking and especially use the *duʿā* you were taught by your guide (*murshid, pir* or shaykh).

2) ***Baʿd al-adhān.*** After the *adhān* has been called.

3) ***Bayn al-adhān wa 'l-iqāmah.*** Between the *adhān* and *iqāmah,* the time when you wait about five minutes after the calling of *adhān* just before the *iqāmah.*

4) ***Adbār aṣ-ṣalāt al-maktubāt.*** After the *farḍ* prayers.

5) ***Wa ʿinda ṣuʿūdi ʾl-imām yawmi ʾl-jumʿah ʿala ʾl-mimbar ḥattā taqḍī aṣ-ṣalāt min dhālika ʾl-yawm.*** On Friday when the *imām* goes up on the *minbar* to give his *khuṭbah*. Make *duʿā* through your heart and think about it until the *khuṭbah* and the prayer is finished.

6) ***Wa ākhiru saʿatin baʿd al-ʿasr.*** The last hour after Ṣalāt al-ʿAṣr, one hour before Maghrib.

The one thing all of these times have in common is *khushūʿ*, sincerity in the heart, which means to focus well on your *duʿā* despite the whispers of shaytan. The best *duʿā* in these six times is the *duʿā* made from a broken heart, in a state of helplessness and weakness, between the Hands of Allah, knowing that you are at His Door. In order for your *duʿā* to be accepted, turn toward your Lord in humility, face the *qiblah*, and ask Him!

2

ادب الطلب من الله

The Etiquette of Asking Allah

As for anything in this world, you must use the correct manners and way of approach in order to reach what you are seeking, when you want to ask Allah. Thus, the scholars and the saints, *Awlīyā* have come up with the conditions for the *duʿā* to be acceptable to Allah, beyond simply asking. These conditions are:

- The seeker should be in state of purity (*ṭahārah*), meaning having *wuḍū*.
- To sit facing *qiblah*.
- To praise Allah and thank Him.
- To make *ṣalawāt* on the Prophet ﷺ.
- To begin your *duʿā* with:

بِسْمِ اللهِ الرَّحْمنِ الرَّحيمِ والحَمْدُ للهِ رَبِّ العالمين.

وَ الصَّلاةُ والسَّلامُ عَلَي اَشْرَفِ المُرسَلِينَ سيدنا مُحَمَدٍ

وَعَلَىَ آلِهِ وصَحْبِهِ أَجْمَعِين

Bismillāhi 'r-Raḥmāni 'r-Raḥīm alḥamdulillāhi rabbi 'l-ʿālamīn wa 'ṣ-ṣalātu wa 's-salāmu ʿalā ashrafi 'l-mursalīn Sayyīdinā Muḥammadin wa ʿalā ālihi wa ṣaḥbihi ajmaʿīn...

then continue with your personal request.

This is the *adab*, good conduct, acceptable to enter in the Divine Presence of Allah ﷻ so that the Door will be opened,

❖ End your *duʿā* with:

سُبْحَانَ رَبِّكَ رَبِّ الْعِزَّةِ عَمَّا يَصِفُونَ ۞

وَسَلَامٌ عَلَى الْمُرْسَلِينَ ۞ وَالْحَمْدُ للهِ رَبِّ الْعَالَمِينَ ۞

رَبَنَا تَقَبَل مِنَّا بِحُرمَةِ مَن أَنزَلتَ عَليهِ سِر

سُورَةِ الفَاتِحَة

Subḥāna rabbika rabbi 'l-ʿizzati ʿammā yaṣifūn wa salāmun ʿalā 'l-mursalīn wa 'l-ḥamdulillāhi rabbi 'l-ʿālamīn. Rabbanā taqabbal minnā bi ḥurmati man anzalta ʿalayhi sirri Sūrat al-Fātiḥa.

Glory be to Your Lord, the Lord of Power, above what they describe! And peace be upon the Messengers. Praise belongs to God, the Lord of the Worlds. O our Lord accept from us for the sake of the one on whom you revealed secret of the Opening Chapter of the Quran.

❖ Close with Sūrat al-Fātiḥa:

After thanking Allah, praising the Prophet ﷺ, asking through the means of the Prophet ﷺ, coming to the Divine Presence, entering and asking through Allah's Beautiful Names and Attributes and through His Divine Oneness, now the key point is to end it with *Sūrat al-Fātiḥa.* Finished!

الْفَاتِحَةُ لِمَا قُرِئَتْ لَهُ

The Prophet ﷺ said:

> The Fātiḥa is for whatever it is read.[1]

And this is confirmed by the hadith:

عَنْ طَلْحَةَ بْنِ عَمْرٍو ، قَالَ : سَمِعْتُ عَطَاءً ، يَقُول:

" إِذَا أَرَدْتَ حَاجَةً ، فَاقْرَأْ بِفَاتِحَةِ الْكِتَابِ حَتَّى تَخْتِمَهَا ،

تُقْضَى إِنْ شَاءَ اللهُ. "

From Ṭalḥa ibn 'Umra'u that he heard 'Aṭā ﷺ say:

[1] Bayhaqī in *Shu'ab al-Imān* from Jābir.

"When anyone has a need to fulfill, then read al-Fātiḥa up to the end, it will be taken care of if Allah wills."[2]

❖ Wrap your *du'ā* with charity:

For a *du'ā* to be accepted, you must bring a *ṣadaqa* in front of (to precede) your *du'ā*. You have to give before or after the *du'ā*, as Allah ﷻ said to the Prophet ﷺ:

خُذْ مِنْ أَمْوَالِهِمْ صَدَقَةً تُطَهِّرُهُمْ وَتُزَكِّيهِم بِهَا وَصَلِّ عَلَيْهِمْ إِنَّ صَلَاتَكَ سَكَنٌ لَّهُمْ وَاللَّهُ سَمِيعٌ عَلِيمٌ

Take alms of their wealth, from which you may purify them and make them grow, and pray for them. Verily, your prayer is an assuagement for them. Allah is Hearer, Knower.[3]

If you truly want something to be done from your *du'ā* give *ṣadaqa*. You cannot come to the door without a gift; you don't come to visit someone without a bringing chocolate or something sweet. You don't bring salt. "Take *ṣadaqa* from them to purify them and clean them," and then it is the responsibility of the Prophet ﷺ to purify and clean them and then pray and ask on their behalf. And that is one of the meanings of intercession.

---

[2] *Al-Maqāsid al-Ḥasanah* of as-Sakhāwī. Abī Shaykh in *Kitāb al-Thawāb*.

[3] Sūrat at-Tawbah, 9:103.

Why do you pay the doctor when you visit him? He charges you before you leave; Allah likes you to give *ṣadaqa* in His Way. Give one euro, one pound, or one dollar in the box in your *masjid* or make a sacrifice and feed orphans or poor people. Give blankets or Holy Qur'an to people who cannot afford it. You have to give something by means of which you will be cured. *Shukran li ḥasānatihi...* Allah makes your *duʿā* accepted, thanking you for the *ṣadaqa* you have given. We have to thank Allah, but He is so generous and merciful with us, saying, "O My servant! You made *duʿā* and on top of that you gave *ṣadaqa*. I am going to give you, bless you, thank you, and raise you higher."

Duʿā done in the way that we described will never be rejected! This way *duʿā* is accepted immediately and if you give no charity, you don't know if it will be accepted.

❖ Supplicate in a Place of Blessings

There are holy places which are far better for making *duʿā*:

كُلَّمَا دَخَلَ عَلَيْهَا زَكَرِيَّا الْمِحْرَابَ وَجَدَ عِندَهَا رِزْقاً قَالَ يَا مَرْيَمُ أَنَّى لَكِ هَـذَا قَالَتْ هُوَ مِنْ عِندِ اللّهِ إنَّ اللّهَ يَرْزُقُ مَن يَشَاء بِغَيْرِ حِسَابٍ

Whenever he (Zakarīya) entered her prayer niche, he found with her provision. He said, "O Mary! From where does this come to you?" She said, "From Allah, for Allah provides sustenance to whom He pleases without measure."[4]

It is clear that every time Zakarīya ﷺ entered the niche of Maryam ؏ he found sustenance there. Why? Because of her *duʿā* and purity, Allah was sending physical and spiritual sustenance from Heavens to her and her place became holy. So Sayyīdinā Zakarīya ﷺ was ninety-nine years old and had no children. How many *duʿā*s had he made, always asking to have a child? But his *duʿā* was accepted when he entered the niche of Sayyida Maryam ؏, where:

$$\text{هُنَالِكَ دَعَا زَكَرِيَّا رَبَّهُ قَالَ رَبِّ هَبْ لِي مِن لَّدُنْكَ ذُرِّيَّةً طَيِّبَةً إِنَّكَ سَمِيعُ الدُّعَاء}$$

In that self-same place, Zakarīya prayed unto his Sustainer, saying: "O my Sustainer! Bestow upon me [too], out of Thy grace, the gift of goodly offspring; for Thou, indeed, hearest all prayer."[5]

He knew it had become a holy place. That is why *ʿulamā* say that *Awlīyāullāh*'s places, as Sayyida

---

[4] Sūrat Āli-ʿImrān, 3:37.
[5] Sūrat Āli-ʿImrān, 3:38.

Maryam is not a prophet, but she is a *walīya,* so her place became a holy place from the immense *tajallī,* manifestation of Allah's Light and Allah's Beautiful Names and Attributes on that place and upon her.

❖ Seek someone pious to make *duʿā*:

It is highly recommended that when you need a *duʿā,* go to those whom you know are sincere servants of Allah as they have been given authorization from their guides, like the Ṣaḥāba were given from Prophet ﷺ and like *a'immah* were given from Ṣaḥāba and like *Awlīyāullāh* were given from *a'immah,* so you go to them and they make *duʿā* for you and you see that their *duʿā* is completely accepted.

I give you an example. There is a man in London married for ten years, whom I know very well. He came to me and said, "We have no children."

I said, "Allah will give you a child next year when we see you, *Inshā-Allah.*"

In my pocket I had a KitKat chocolate bar and I read Sūrat *al-Fātiḥa* on it and said, "You eat half, let your wife eat half and *inshā-Allah* you will have a child." I came the next year but there was no child and I didn't say anything, I kept quiet. The following year I went and his wife had a child! He told me, "*Yā Shaykh*! When you left and one year had passed, I didn't remember you gave me the chocolate; it was in the drawer! So when we were cleaning I found the KitKat and broke it in half. We each ate half and then after that we had a child."

عَنْ أَنَسِ بْنِ مَالِكٍ، قَالَ : سَمِعْتُ رَسُولَ اللهِ، ﷺ، يَقُولُ
:رُبَّ أَشْعَثَ أَغْبَرَ ذِي طِمْرَيْنِ لاَ يُؤْبَهُ لَهُ لَوْ أَقْسَمَ عَلَى اللهِ
لَأَبَرَّهُ .

Anas related that the Prophet said:

> There may be a disheveled, dusty person who, if he swears an oath by Allah, Allah will fulfill it.[6]

It means Allah will not reject anyone through his outside appearance because He looks only at the inside.

عَنْ أَبِي هُرَيْرَةَ قَالَ قَالَ رَسُولُ اللهِ ﷺ إِنَّ اللهَ لاَ يَنْظُرُ إِلَى
صُوَرِكُمْ وَأَمْوَالِكُمْ وَلَكِنْ يَنْظُرُ إِلَى قُلُوبِكُمْ وَأَعْمَالِكُمْ

Abū Hurayrah related that the Prophet said:

---

[6] Bukhārī, Muslim, *Jami'a at-Tirmidhī, Sunan Abū Dāwūd, Sunan Ibn Mājah, Sunan al-Nisā'ī, Musnad* of Ahmad, *al-Mustadrak* of al-Ḥākim and others.

Verily Allah does not look at your bodies nor at your appearances but He looks at your hearts.⁷

Similarly, one may go to the grave of such pious persons: Prophet Muḥammad ﷺ, other prophets and messengers, Ṣaḥāba ؓ and *Awlīyāullāh* and make *duʿā* in their presence, for they are present with Allah ﷻ, and being with them when asking is like presenting your *duʿā* to the Divine Presence through their intercession.⁸ Allah said about them:

---

⁷ Muslim.

⁸ These selected authentic reports (among many others) from our pious predecessors among the *Salaf al-Ṣāliḥ* which show that contrary to the claims of Wahhabis, the Ummah acts lawfully when visiting the graves of *Awlīyā* for the sake of blessing, intercession and benefit just as taught by the Ṣaḥābī ʿUbāda ibn al-Ṣāmiṭ ؓ.

(i) "The early Muslims would come to the grave of Abū Ayyūb al-Anṣārī to pray for rain." – Narrated from Mujāhid by Abū Nuʿaym al-Asfahānī in *Ḥilyat ul-Awlīyā wa ṭabaqāt al-asfīyā*, Ibn al-Jawzī in *Ṣifat al-Ṣafwā* and al-Dhahabī in *Siyār Aʿlām al-Nubalāʾ*.

(ii) "We used to seek blessing (*tabarruk*) through the grave of Abū al-Fatḥ al-Qawāsī." Narrated from al-Dāraqutnī by Abū Nuʿaym al-Asfahānī in *Ḥilyat*, Ibn al-Jawzī in *Ṣifat al-Ṣafwā* and al-Dhahabī in *Siyār Aʿlām al-Nubalāʾ*.

(iii) "The grave of Maʿrūf al-Karkhī is a tried and proven cure-all (*al-tiryāq al-mujarrab*)." – Narrated from Ibrāhīm al-Ḥarbī (one of the two most senior companions of Imām Aḥmad ibn Ḥanbal) by Ibn al-Jawzī in *Ṣifat al-Ṣafwā* and al-Dhahabī in *Siyār*.

(iv) "I heard al-Shāfiʿī say that he would come to the grave of Abū Ḥanīfa in Baghdad and use him as his intermediary for the fulfillment of his

وَلَا تَقُولُوا لِمَنْ يُقْتَلُ فِي سَبِيلِ اللهِ أَمْوَاتٌ بَلْ أَحْيَاء وَلَكِن لَا تَشْعُرُونَ

And say not of those who are slain in God's cause, "They are dead": nay, they are alive, but you perceive it not.[9]

And here we cite what Īmām Mullah al-Qārī's recommendation on how to ask by means of the prophets, Companions and *Awlīyā*:

> Whenever you visit the grave of a prophet or a *wali* or a scholar or those below them in status, and you are in great distress, and you wish

needs." Narrated from ʿAlī bin Maymūn by al-Khatīb in *Tārīkh Baghdād* and al-Haytamī in *al-Khayrāt al-Ḥisān.*

(v) The same is narrated through various reports in relation to the grave of Īmām al-Bukhārī as in Ibn al-Subkī's *Ṭabaqāt al-Shafiʿīyya al-Kubrā* and elsewhere.

(vi) The grave of Īmām Aḥmad in Baghdad received countless visitors for *tawassul* and *tabarruk* among the early Hanbalis. The Hanbali Qāḍī Muḥammad Abū ʿAlī al-Hāshimī used to kiss the foot of the grave of Īmām Aḥmad as narrated by Ibn Abī Yaʿalā in *Ṭabaqāt al-Ḥanābila* as did many others. Ibrāhīm al-Harbī saw Īmām Aḥmad in a dream and asked him: "How come people only kiss your grave and no other grave?" Īmām Aḥmad replied: "Because I have with me some hair of the Prophet ﷺ." Ibn al-Jawzī narrated it in *Manāqib al-Īmām Aḥmad.* Finally, the Hanbali Ḥāfiẓ of Hadith al-Ḍiyā' al-Maqdisī in his book *al-Hikāyat al-Manthūra* narrated that his teacher the Ḥāfiẓ Abd al-Ghanī al-Maqdisī travelled from Damascus to Baghdad and wiped the grave of Īmām Aḥmad with his face and body seeking a cure from abscesses he was suffering from.

[9] Sūrat al-Baqara (The Cow) 2:154.

for the spirit (*rūḥ*) of the person in that grave be present with you so that you can complain to them of what is affecting you—meaning you complain through just being there or verbatim, so that they will intercede for you in the Presence of the Supreme Owner of all, then He will suffice you against all that worries you and cure you of your disease: Recite *Qul hūwa Allāhu āḥad* ten times; and if you first start with the Heart of the Qur'an—I mean Surah Yāsīn—it is better and faster, then the last three Suras three times each, then the Fātiḥa, the beginning and end of Sūrat al-Baqara, and the Beautiful Names. Then you close your eyes and summon up all your heart to be present and say: *Lā ilāha il-Llāh* three times, then ALLĀH three times lengthening the final A. Then you stay silent for a while and then you say: *Salām ʿalaykum* and the mercy of Allah and His blessings, O *Sayyīdī* So-and-so! or: O Shaykh! or: O my teacher! or: O Messenger of Allah ﷺ! And you present your problems to the one you are visiting. He will lift them up by the gift of the Almighty Concealer of faults, through the intercession fo the one in that grave. This is one of the greatest benefits to know.[10]

---

[10] Mullah al-Qārī's words as cited by Yūsuf an-Nabahānī in his book *Shawāhid al-Ḥaqq* his commentary on Ibn al-Jazarī's *al-Ḥisn al-Ḥasīn.*

And from Allah is all success.

3

الدعاء باسم الله الأعظم

SUPPLICATIONS CONTAINING ALLAH'S GREATEST NAME

Any *duʿā* you make with *Ismullāhi 'l-ʿAẓam*, the Greatest Name of Allah ﷻ, will be like a sword that will cut your problems immediately and bring you towards the Divine Presence! We can at least take one of these *duʿās*, perhaps the easiest one for recitation, learn it and recite it. There are also verses of the Holy Qur'an that contain the *Ismullāhi 'l-ʿAẓam* such as *awā'il as-sūwar*, the beginning of all *Sūrahs*. Also, if you read:

قُلْ هُوَ اللهُ أَحَدٌ ۝ اللهُ الصَّمَدُ ۝ لَمْ يَلِدْ وَلَمْ يُولَدْ ۝ وَلَمْ يَكُنْ لَهُ كُفُوًا أَحَدٌ ۝

"*Qul hūwa Allāhu āḥad, Allāhu 'ṣ-Ṣamad, lam yalid wa lam yūlad, wa lam yakun lahu kufūwan āḥad*" (*Sūrat al-Ikhlāṣ)* three times it will be as if you have read the whole Qur'an (as the Prophet ﷺ said, "*Sūrat al-Ikhlāṣ* equals one-third of the Holy Qur'an"), which means *Ismullāhi 'l-ʿAẓam* is included.

1) Two Verses in the Holy Qur'an:

As related by Tirmidhī, Asmā bint Yazīd ﵂ reported the Prophet ﷺ said, "Allah's Greatest Name is in these two verses." Anyone who has a problem and makes *duʿā* through these two verses that contain *Ismullāhi 'l-ʿAẓam*, Allah ﷻ will accept what he wants!

وَإِلَٰهُكُمْ إِلَٰهٌ وَاحِدٌ لا إِلَٰهَ إِلا هُوَ الرَّحْمَٰنُ

Wa ilāhukum ilāhun wāḥidun lā ilāha illa Hūwa 'r-Raḥmānu 'r-Raḥīm.

And your God is one God: there is no god but He, the Compassionate, the Merciful.[19]

الم . اللهُ لا إِلَٰهَ إِلا هُوَ الْحَيُّ الْقَيُّومُ

Alif. Lām. Mīm. Allāhu lā ilāha illa Huwa 'l-Hayyu 'l- Qayyūm.

Allah, there is no god but He, the Living, the Eternal.[20]

---

[19] Sūrat al-Baqarah, 2:163.

[20] Sūrat Āli-ʿImrān, 3:1-2.

2) *Duʿā* of Sayyīdinā Yūnus ﷷ and to Die as a Martyr:

Allah ﷻ sent Sayyīdinā Yūnus ﷷ to a nation of 100,000 people to call them to Him. He called and called, and they didn't listen to him and so he ran away (seeking solitude in Allah). In order to teach him a lesson, Allah ﷻ ordered the whale to swallow him.

عَن سَعْدِ بْنِ أَبِي وَقَّاصٍ عَنِ النَّبِيِّ ﷺ قَالَ : دَعْوَةُ ذِي النُّونِ ، إِذْ دَعَا وَهُوَ فِي بَطْنِ الْحُوتِ ﴿ لَا إِلَهَ إِلَّا أَنْتَ سُبْحَانَكَ إِنِّي كُنْتُ مِنَ الظَّالِمِينَ ﴾ إِنَّهُ لَمْ يَدْعُ بِهَا مُسْلِمٌ فِي شَيْءٍ قَطُّ إِلَّا اسْتَجَابَ اللهُ لَهُ.

The Prophet ﷺ said that Sayyīdinā Yunus ﷷ used to make a *duʿā* in the belly of the whale. That *duʿā* is a verse in the Holy Qur'an. But Sayyīdinā Yunus ﷷ didn't say it only once, he was saying it continuously on his breathing in and breathing out, until Allah's test finished and the whale threw him out. So Allah ﷻ is telling us to recite it like Dhu 'n-Nūn ﷷ, Sayyīdinā Yūnus ﷷ and you will get the reward from Him in health and wealth!

The Prophet ﷺ said, "In anything that you ask, in illness or need, or anything at all, if you recite that verse Allah will respond to you and answer you." That *duʿā* is:

لَا إِلَهَ إِلَّا أَنْتَ سُبْحَانَكَ إِنِّي كُنْتُ مِنَ الظَّالِمِينَ

Lā ilāha illa anta innī kuntu min aẓ-ẓālimīn.

There is no god but You. Glory be to You! Verily, I have been among the wrongdoers.[21]

عَن سَعْدِ بْنِ أَبِي وَقَّاصٍ أَنَّهُ سَمِعَ النَّبِيَّ ﷺ وَهُوَ يَقُولُ : هَلْ أَدُلُّكُمْ عَلَى اسْمِ اللهِ الْأَعْظَمِ ؟ دُعَاءِ يُونُسَ ، فَقَالَ رَجُلٌ : يَا رَسُولَ اللهِ ، هَلْ كَانَ لِيُونُسَ خَاصَّةً ؟ فَقَالَ أَلَا تَسْمَعُ قَوْلَهُ ﴿ فَاسْتَجَبْنَا لَهُ وَنَجَّيْنَاهُ مِنَ الْغَمِّ وَكَذَلِكَ نُنْجِي الْمُؤْمِنِينَ ﴾ فَأَيُّمَا مُسْلِمٍ دَعَا بِهَا فِي مَرَضِهِ أَرْبَعِينَ مَرَّةً فَمَاتَ فِي مَرَضِهِ ذَلِكَ أُعْطِيَ أَجْرَ شَهِيدٍ ، وَإِنْ بَرِئَ بَرِئَ مَغْفُورًا لَهُ.

One time the Prophet ﷺ asked the Ṣaḥāba ﵁, "Do you want me to teach you the Greatest Name of Allah (which, if you use it, Allah will grant whatever you ask immediately without restriction)? It is the *duʿā* of Sayyīdinā Yūnus ﵇." One *Sahābah* ﵁ asked, "Is that private to Yūnus ﵇?" and the Prophet ﷺ said, "Did you not hear Allah's Word?

فَاسْتَجَبْنَا لَهُ وَنَجَّيْنَاهُ مِنَ الْغَمِّ وَكَذَلِكَ نُنجِي الْمُؤْمِنِينَ

> *'And so We responded to him and delivered him from his distress, for thus do We deliver all who have faith.'*"[22]

---

[21] *Jamiʿah at-Tirmidhī* and *Saḥīḥ* of al-Ḥākim, from Saʿd Ibn Abī Waqqās ﵁.

[22] Sūrat al-Anbīyā, 21:88.

and any Muslim who recites this verse during his illness from which he dies, if he recited it forty times then he will die as a *shahīd*! *Wa in burīya burīya maghfūran lah,* and if he didn't die he will be cured and he will be forgiven."[23]

It means, "We accepted his *duʿā* and We saved him from all *ghamm*, miseries!" So if you read the Holy Qur'an it will save you. People were running to die as *shahīd* (martyrs) in the time of the Prophet ﷺ but with one *duʿā* they could achieve that, and that is:

لَّا إِلَهَ إِلَّا أَنتَ سُبْحَانَكَ إِنِّي كُنتُ مِنَ الظَّالِمِينَ

Lā ilāha illa Anta! Subhānaka innī kuntu min aẓ-ẓālimīn!
There is no god except You! Limitless are You in your Glory! Verily I am among the oppressors!

3) Sahābah's Duʿā for Specific Needs

Hadith of ʿAbdullāh Ibn Buraydah ؓ

عَنْ عَبْدِ اللَّهِ بْنِ بُرَيْدَةَ عَنْ أَبِيهِ أَنَّ رَسُولَ اللَّهِ ﷺ سَمِعَ رَجُلاً يَقُولُ : اللَّهُمَّ إِنِّي أَسْأَلُكَ بِأَنِّي أَشْهَدُ أَنَّكَ أَنْتَ اللَّهُ لَا إِلَهَ إِلَّا أَنْتَ ، الْأَحَدُ الصَّمَدُ الَّذِي لَمْ يَلِدْ وَلَمْ يُولَدْ وَلَمْ يَكُنْ لَهُ كُفُوًا أَحَدٌ ، فَقَالَ : لَقَدْ سَأَلَ

---

[23] Sūrat al-Anbīyā 21:87.

اللهَّ بِالِاسْمِ الَّذِي إِذَا سُئِلَ بِهِ أَعْطَى ، وَإِذَا دُعِيَ بِهِ أَجَابَ وَفِي لَفْظٍ :
لَقَدْ سَأَلْتَ اللهَّ بِاسْمِهِ الْأَعْظَمِ.

ʿAbdullāh Ibn Buraydah ؓ related from his father that the Prophet ﷺ heard a man reciting a *duʿā* about which he said, "That man has asked Allah ﷻ with the Name through which if anyone asks anything by it he will be granted and if he prays in that way He will respond." And in one narration he added, "verily he has asked by Allah by means of His greatest name."

The *duʿā* is:

Allāhumma innī as'aluka, bi-annī ash-hadu annaka anta 'Llāhu lā ilāha illa anta 'l-aḥadu 'ṣ-ṣamad, alladhī lam yalid wa lam yūlad wa lam yakun lahu kufūwan aḥad!

O Allah! I am asking you and witness that you are Allah! There is none to be worshipped except Allah, The Unique that is Not Dependent on Anyone and The One Who does not give birth nor is born and there is no one associated with Him.[24]

Hadith of Anas ibn Mālik ؓ

عَنْ أَنَسٍ ؓ ، قَالَ : كُنْتُ جَالِسًا مَعَ رَسُولِ اللهَّ ﷺ فِي الْحَلْقَةِ ، وَرَجُلٌ قَائِمٌ يُصَلِّي فَلَمَّا رَكَعَ وَسَجَدَ جَلَسَ وَتَشَهَّدَ ، ثُمَّ دَعَا

[24] *Saḥīḥ Ibn Ḥibbān.*

فَقَالَ : " اللَّهُمَّ إِنِّي أَسْأَلُكَ بِأَنَّ لَكَ الْحَمْدَ لَا إِلَهَ إِلَّا أَنْتَ ، الْمَنَّانُ يَا بَدِيعَ السَّمَاوَاتِ وَالْأَرْضِ ، يَا ذَا الْجَلَالِ وَالْإِكْرَامِ ، يَا حَيُّ يَا قَيُّومُ ، إِنِّي أَسْأَلُكَ ، فَقَالَ رَسُولُ اللَّهِ ﷺ : أَتَدْرُونَ بِمَا دَعَا ؟ فَقَالُوا : اللَّهُ وَرَسُولُهُ أَعْلَمُ ، قَالَ : وَالَّذِي نَفْسِي بِيَدِهِ لَقَدْ دَعَا اللَّهَ بِاسْمِهِ الْعَظِيمِ الَّذِي إِذَا دُعِيَ بِهِ أَجَابَ ، وَإِذَا سُئِلَ بِهِ أَعْطَى."

It is narrated that Anas ibn Mālik ☙ said, "I was sitting with the Prophet ☙ and a man was offering prayer. He then made a *duʿā* (see below)," [and for sure that man began his *duʿā* with"*Bismillāhi 'r-Rahmāni 'r-Rahīm, alhamdulillāhi rabbi 'l-ʿalamīn wa 'ṣ-ṣalātu wa 's-salāmu ʿalā ashrafi 'l-mursalīn Sayyīdinā Muḥammadin wa ʿalā ālihi wa ṣahbihi ajmaʿīn.*"] The Prophet ☙ then said, "He has asked Allah using His Greatest Name. If you call upon Allah through that Name He will respond and if you ask Allah through that Name He will give!"[25]

This is the *duʿā*:

---

[25] Āḥmad in his *Musnad*, al-Ḥākim, ibn Hibbān in his *Saḥīḥ*, Imām Bayhaqī in *al-Asmāi waʾṣ-Ṣiffāt*, *al-Duʿā* of aṭ-Ṭabarānī and others.

$$\text{اللَّهُمَّ إِنِّي أَسْأَلُكَ بِأَنَّ لَكَ الْحَمْدَ لَا إِلَهَ إِلَّا أَنْتَ، الْمَنَّانُ يَا بَدِيعَ السَّمَاوَاتِ وَالْأَرْضِ، يَا ذَا الْجَلَالِ وَالْإِكْرَامِ، يَا حَيُّ يَا قَيُّومُ إِني أسألك،}$$

Allahumma innī as'aluka bi-anna laka 'l-hamdu lā ilāha illā anta 'l-Mannānu Yā Badī' as-samāwāti wa 'l-arḍi, Yā Dha 'l-Jalāli wa 'l-Ikrām, Yā Ḥayyu, Yā Qayyūm innī as'aluka.

O Allah! We ask of You by virtue of all praise being to You, there is no God worthy of worship but You alone. There is no partner for You, the Beneficent, Creator of the Heavens and the Earth. O Lord of Majesty and Bounty! O Alive Self-Subsisting One! I ask of You.

4) Overcoming Tribulation

Raising One's Head Skywards

As related by Miqdād ◈ and Sayyida 'Āishā ◈, whenever a burden or a difficult matter came on him, the Prophet ◈ would raise his head towards the sky.[26] Usually we look at our hands when making *du'ā*, but when there is a big affliction, rather than showing humbleness you raise our hands high, saying, "*Yā Rabbī! Yā Rabbī!*" to show that you are really in need.

---

[26] Miqdād's ◈ hadith is related in *Saḥīḥ Muslim* and Sayyida 'Āishā's hadith is related by Īmām Bukhārī.

عَن أَبِي هُرَيْرَة ﷺ أَنَّ النَّبِيَّ ﷺ كَانَ إِذَا أَهَمَّهُ الأَمْرُ رَفَعَ رَأْسَهُ إِلَى السَّمَاءِ ، وَإِذَا اجْتَهَدَ فِي الدُّعَاءِ ، قَالَ : يَا حَيُّ يَا قَيُّومُ

It was related by Abū Hurayrah ﷺ that whenever a burden or a difficult matter came upon him, the Prophet ﷺ would raise his head towards the sky, and when he strove hard in invocation, he would say: *"Yā Ḥayyu, Yā Qayyūm!"*[27]

Hadith of Anas ﷺ

عن أَنَس بْن مَالِكٍ ﷺ؛ قال: كَانَ النَّبِيُّ ﷺ إِذَا حَزَبَهُ أَمْرٌ قَالَ : يَا حَيُّ يَا قَيُّومُ بِرَحْمَتِكَ أَسْتَغِيثُ

As related by Anas bin Malik ﷺ whenever the Prophet ﷺ went into a difficulty he raised his hands and said:

Yā Ḥayyu, Yā Qayyūm! Bi-raḥmatika astaghīth.

O Living One, O Self-Subsisting One! With Your Mercy I seek Your help![28]

---

[27] *Saḥīḥ Tirmidhī.*

[28] *Saḥīḥ Tirmidhī.*

4

ادعية المبتلي

SUPPLICATIONS FOR CALAMITIES

قَالَ ابْنُ مَسْعُودٍ ﷺ: مَا كَرَبَ نَبِيٌّ مِنَ الْأَنْبِيَاءِ، إِلَّا اسْتَغَاثَ بِالتَّسْبِيحِ.

Ibn Mas'ūd said, "Anyone of the prophets who felt an affliction coming was able to take it away by reciting *tasbīḥ*."[29]

You may recite any *tasbīḥ* that comes to your heart from Allah's Beautiful Names and Attributes. We believe that every *du'ā* has an effect and a cure, but if we don't know

---

[29] Related by Ibn Qayyim al-Jawzīyya in his *al-Jawāb al-Kāfi liman s'al 'an al-dawā' ash-shāfi*.

any *duʿās,* through our hearts with Allah's Beautiful Names and Attributes, Allah will accept.

There are four different calamitous situations for which different *duʿās* apply:

Prevention of Affliction

عَن عَلِيِّ بْنِ أَبِي طَالِبٍ ﷛ قَالَ : عَلَّمَنِي رَسُولُ اللهِ ﷺ إِذَا نَزَلَ بِي كَرْبٌ أَنْ أَقُولَ : لَا إِلَهَ إِلَّا اللهُ الْحَلِيمُ الْكَرِيمُ ، سُبْحَانَ اللهِ وَتَبَارَكَ اللهُ رَبُّ الْعَرْشِ الْعَظِيمِ ، وَالْحَمْدُ للهِ رَبِّ الْعَالَمِينَ .

Sayyīdinā ʿAlī ﷛ said, "When an affliction came down or I was put in a difficulty, Prophet ﷺ taught me to say:

Lā ilāha illa-Llāh al-Ḥalīm al-Karīm, subḥān-Allahi wa tabārakallāhu Rabbu'l-ʿArshi 'l-ʿAẓīm, w'alḥamdulillāhi Rabbi 'l-ʿālamīn.

There is none worthy of worship except Allah the Most Forbearing, the Most Generous! Glorious is He and Blessed be He the Lord of the Great Throne, and all praises be to the Lord of the Worlds."[30]

Reciting that will throw away a bad happening. This *duʿā* prevents affliction from entering through a particular door. How many doors are there in the human body and how many are we going to close? There are three trillion doors in the body, a door on every cell in the

---

[30] Āḥmad in his *Musnad.*

body! If one cell is hurting the whole body hurts, as mentioned by the Prophet ﷺ that if a part of the body is hurting, the whole body will ache. So how can we close these doors? Allah ﷻ is soft and patient with us; He will accept your repentance.

When Afflicted with Calamity

Hadith of the Thief

Who doesn't have afflictions? If you have a nice life, you still may have too many sins. Whether you have a problem or not, if you make this *duʿā* Allah ﷻ will shut that door of sickness.

It is related by Sayyīdinā al-Ḥasan ؓ, grandson of the Prophet ﷺ, from Ibn Abī ad-Dunyā in his book *Kitāb al-Mujābīn, Book of Those Whose Duʿās Allah Accepted*:

> There was a *Ṣaḥābī* ؓ from the *Anṣār* in the time of the Prophet ﷺ who was a merchant who made good money. He traveled a lot and people invested their money with him and he brought good profit. One day he was traveling with some money and a thief stopped him. It was difficult to see his face as it was covered, and as he drew out his sword he said, "Put out all the money you have and on top of that, I am going to kill you, I will not leave you!" The *Ṣaḥābī* ؓ said, "Take the money. What do you need from my blood?" The thief answered, "I

am taking your money and I will also kill you." The *Ṣaḥābī* said, "If you don't want to leave me alone, give me permission to pray four *raka'ats* before I die." "Pray as much as you like," said the thief, "I will kill you right here but if you want time to pray, I will give it to you."

So that *Ṣaḥābī* ﷺ made *wuḍū,* prayed four *raka'ats* and then in the last *sajda* recited this *du'ā*:

يَا وَدُودُ ، يَا ذَا الْعَرْشِ الْمَجِيدِ ، يَا فَعَّالُ لِمَا تُرِيدُ ، أَسْأَلُكَ بِعِزِّكَ الَّذِي لَا يُرَامُ ، وَمُلْكِكَ الَّذِي لَا يُضَامُ ، وَبِنُورِكَ الَّذِي مَلَأَ أَرْكَانَ عَرْشِكَ ، أَنْ تَكْفِيَنِي شَرَّ هَذَا اللِّصِّ ، يَا مُغِيثُ أَغِثْنِي ، يَا مُغِيثُ أَغِثْنِي ، يَا مُغِيثُ أَغِثْنِي

Yā Wadūd, Yā Wadūd! Yā Dhal-'Arshi 'l-Majīd! Yā fa'ālan limā turīd! As'aluka bi 'izzika 'Lladhī lā yurām wa bi-mulkika 'Lladhī lā yudām wa bi-nūrika 'Lladhī malā'a arkāna 'arshika an takfiyanī sharra hādha 'Lliṣ. Yā Mughīthu, aghithnī! Yā Mughīthu, aghithnī! Yā Mughīthu, aghithnī!

O Loving One! O Lord of the Glorified Throne! O You Who does what He wants! I ask You through Your Might which cannot be harmed, and Your Dominion which cannot be defeated, and Your Light which filled the pillars of Your Thrown, that You protect me from the evil of this thief! O Savior from Calamity, save me! O Savior from Calamity, save me! O Savior from Calamity, save me!

As soon as he finished his *duʿā,* a knight began to approach with a *harbah,* big spear in his hand. He had it placed on the ears of his horse. When the thief looked at him, he approached him to fight. The knight killed the thief with just one strike. Then he came to the Companion of the Prophet ﷺ and said, "Stand up." The *Ṣaḥābī* ؓ said, "For the sake of Allah ﷻ and Prophet ﷺ, may Allah give you my life! Who are you? Allah has saved me today by your hands!" He said, "I am an angel from the angels of the Fourth Heaven. When you made that *duʿā,* after the first part I heard the doors of heavens cracking with a loud noise, *samʿitu bi abwābi samā ar-rabiʿa qāqā.* Then after the second part of your *duʿā, dajja kabīra,* the Inhabitants of the heavens heard a lot of noise. Then after the third part of your *duʿā,* a voice came to me saying, 'Go and help that person in distress!' I asked Allah to give me permission to kill him."

And Sayyīdinā al-Ḥasan ؓ (the *Ṣaḥābī* narrator) said, "Whoever makes *wuḍū,* prays four *rakaʿats* and makes this *duʿā,* Allah will accept it from him regardless if that person has any afflictions or not."[31]

Salvation from Punishment

The Holy Qur'an contains not only *Āyātu 'sh-Shifā*, verses of healing, to cure us, but it also saves us from the greatest sickness and disease, the most frightening element that people, especially *mu'mins*, believers, and Muslims, think about, which is *Jahannam*, Hellfire. *Jahannam*'s punishment is for Muslims and *mu'mins* who committed sins and did not repent! It is Allah's Mercy that He gave us the Holy Qur'an and after every verse of *'adhāb*, punishment, that shows you deserve *Jahannam*, Hellfire, He gave us an *āyah* of *raḥmah*, Mercy. So if you don't read the Holy Qur'an you are stuck, as Holy Qur'an is the way out of punishment and the way into *raḥmah*!

Ease from the Trumpet-Blast

عَنْ أَبِي سَعِيدٍ الْخُدْرِيِّ ، قَالَ : قَالَ رَسُولُ اللَّهِ ﷺ : " كَيْفَ أَنْعَمُ وَقَدِ
الْتَقَمَ صَاحِبُ الْقَرْنِ الْقَرْنَ وَحَنَى جَبْهَتَهُ وَأَصْغَى سَمْعَهُ يَنْتَظِرُ أَنْ

[31] Ibn Abī ad-Dunyā in *Kitāb al-Mujābīn*, (Book of Those Whose Du'ās Allah Accepted).

$$\text{يُؤْمَرَ أَنْ يَنْفُخَ فَيَنْفُخَ "، قَالَ المُسْلِمُونَ : فَكَيْفَ نَقُولُ يَا رَسُولَ اللهِ}$$
$$\text{؟ قَالَ : " قُولُوا : حَسْبُنَا اللهُ وَنِعْمَ الْوَكِيلُ ، تَوَكَّلْنَا عَلَى اللهِ رَبِّنَا ، "}$$

Abū Saʿīd al-Khuḍrī ؓ narrated that the Prophet ﷺ said, "How can I be at ease when the bearer of the Trumpet has put the Trumpet to his lips, has tilted his forehead, is listening out, waiting for the command to blow the Trumpet?" The Ṣaḥāba ؓ asked, 'What should we say, O Messenger of Allah?' The Prophet ﷺ said, 'Say: *Ḥasbun Allāh wa niʿma 'l-wakīl, ʿala-Llāhi tawakkalnā.*'"

"Allah is Sufficient for us, and He is the best Disposer of affairs. Upon Allah we put our trust."[32]

The Prophet ﷺ was saying, "How could I enjoy myself and live happily when Isrāfīl ؑ, the Angel holding the trumpet, is already holding it to his mouth ready to blow on it and when he blows it everything will vanish! I do not know the moment that he will blow in it and whether (our destiny) is to be in Heaven or Hellfire. How am I going to live happily?"

If you really think about it, you will be sitting in a corner crying continuously and repenting--not do anything but to cry. The Prophet ﷺ is the most worried for his *Ummah*, his Community; he does not care for himself, but only for his *Ummah*. That is why Allah ﷻ gave him higher and higher (stations) because he put his *Ummah* in front. If

---

[32] *Jāmiʿ* of at-Tirmidhī.

he is caring for his *Ummah* that they might be punished, then why are we not caring and thinking?

When the *Ṣahābah* ﷺ asked what they should say in order to be saved, the Prophet ﷺ said, "Recite *Ḥasbun Allāh wa niʿma 'l-wakīl, ʿala-Llāhi tawakkalnā,*" which means, "O my Lord! There is no way out of our sins except through You!" That is why we have a daily *wird* to recite one-hundred to one-thousand times, *'Ḥasbun Allāh wa niʿma 'l-wakīl.*" So now is it dangerous (to leave it) or not? Yes!

And for leaving one prayer you will get the juice of Hell-fire! O People! We have to be very careful. What will save us? *Duʿā*! Keep making *duʿā*: *Ḥasbun Allāh wa niʿma 'l-wakīl, ʿala 'Llāhi tawakkalnā. niʿma 'l-mawlā wa niʿma 'n-naṣīr ghufrānaka rabbanā wa ilayka 'l-maṣīr.*

Sultan al-Awlīyā's Prescription for Overall Protection

قَالَ ابْنُ عَبَّاسٍ ﷺ: مَنْ سَمِعَ صَوْتَ الرَّعْدِ فَقَالَ : سُبْحَانَ الَّذِي يُسَبِّحُ الرَّعْدُ بِحَمْدِهِ، وَالْمَلَائِكَةُ مِنْ خِيفَتِهِ وَهُوَ عَلَى كُلِّ شَيْءٍ قَدِيرٌ، فَإِنْ أَصَابَتْهُ صَاعِقَةٌ فَعَلَيَّ دِيَتُهُ.

Sayyīdinā Ibn 'Abbās ؓ said, "Whoever hears thunder and then recites this *du'ā* and he is struck by lightning, I am responsible for his retribution!" Therefore, repeat it all the time!

Subḥān-alladhī yusabbiḥu 'r-ra'du bi-ḥamdihi wa 'l-malā'ikatu min khīfatihi wa hūwa 'alā kulla shay'in qadīr.

Glory is to Him for Whom the thunder exalts His praise, as do the angels, in awe of Him, and He has power over all things.[33]

---

[33] Sa'īd ibn Manṣūr and ibn Mundhir.

دعاء الحاجة

DUʿĀ OF NEED

Duʿā al-Ḥājjah - Supplication of the Blind Man through Intercession of the Prophet ﷺ

Allah ﷻ will not leave anything that He wants to give to humanity without it passing through His Beloved ﷺ. First it has to go through the door, which is Sayyīdinā Muḥammad ﷺ. It must first go through Rasūlullāh ﷺ and then from the Prophet ﷺ it must be divided or reflected to humanity.

عَنْ عُثْمَانَ بْنِ حُنَيْفٍ، أَنَّ رَجُلًا ضَرِيرَ الْبَصَرِ أَتَى النَّبِيَّ ﷺ فَقَالَ: ادْعُ اللهَ أَنْ يُعَافِيَنِي، قَالَ: " إِنْ شِئْتَ دَعَوْتُ لَكَ، وَإِنْ شِئْتَ أَخَّرْتُ ذَاكَ، فَهُوَ خَيْرٌ " . فَقَالَ: " ادْعُهُ، فَأَمَرَهُ أَنْ يَتَوَضَّأَ، فَيُحْسِنَ وُضُوءَهُ، وَيُصَلِّيَ رَكْعَتَيْنِ، وَيَدْعُوَ بِهَذَا الدُّعَاءِ: اللهُمَّ إِنِّي أَسْأَلُكَ، وَأَتَوَجَّهُ إِلَيْكَ بِنَبِيِّكَ مُحَمَّدٍ نَبِيِّ الرَّحْمَةِ، يَا مُحَمَّدُ، إِنِّي تَوَجَّهْتُ بِكَ إِلَى رَبِّي فِي حَاجَتِي هَذِهِ، فَتَقْضِي لِي، اللهُمَّ شَفِّعْهُ فِيَّ "

A blind man came to the Prophet ﷺ. He wanted to come and pray with the Prophet ﷺ but being blind made it is very difficult. He had no one to help take him to be with the Prophet ﷺ. He said, *"Yā Rasūlullāh,* O Messenger of Allah ﷻ! Can you make a *duʿā* that will cure me [from blindness]?" The Prophet ﷺ said to him, "If you wish I will pray for you and if you wish, I can postpone that [you must be patient]?" He said, "Pray for it," because he could not be patient. Then the Prophet ﷺ said, "Go to the place for *wuḍū*, make a perfect ablution and pray two *rakaʿats*, and then make this *duʿā:*

Yā Muḥammad! Innī tawajjahtu bika ilā Rabbī fī ḥājatī hādhihi fa-taqḍī lī. Allāhumma shaffiʿhu fiyya.

"O Muḥammad! I am turning to My Lord, taking you as a means for my request to be granted. O Allah, grant me his intercession. O Allah ﷻ give him authority to intercede for Your honor in Your Presence."

So that blind man went and read it and immediately his sight came back.[34]

When people have problems they should read the *duʿā* that the Prophet ﷺ taught the blind man in order to be given back his sight. If they use that intercessory *duʿā* their problems will be solved.

---

[34] al-Tirmidhī, al-Nasā'ī, al-Bayhaqī, and al-Ṭabarānī all relate this hadith with a sound chain.

اللهُمَّ إِنِّي أَسْأَلُكَ، وَأَتَوَجَّهُ إِلَيْكَ بِنَبِيِّكَ مُحَمَّدٍ نَبِيِّ الرَّحْمَةِ، يَا مُحَمَّدُ، إِنِّي تَوَجَّهْتُ بِكَ إِلَى رَبِّي فِي حَاجَتِي هَذِهِ، فَتَقْضِي لِي، اللهُمَّ شَفِّعْهُ فِيَّ

Allāhuma innī asa'luka wa atawajjahu bi Nabīyyika Muḥammad Nabīyyi 'r-raḥma. Yā Muḥammad! Innī tawajjahtu bika ilā Rabbī fī ḥājati hādhihi fa-taqḍī lī. Allāhumma shaffiʿhu fiyya.

"O Allah, I am asking you and turning to you by means of Your prophet Muḥammad, the prophet of Mercy. O Muḥammad! I am turning to My Lord, taking you as a means for my request to be granted. O Allah, grant me his intercession. O Allah ﷻ give him authority to intercede for Your honor in Your Presence."

سيد الدعاء لشيخ عبد الله الفائز الداغستاني

THE MASTER OF SUPPLICATIONS

of Mawlānā Shaykh ʿAbdullāh al-Fā'iz ad-Dāghestānī (may Allah sanctify his secret)

Grandshaykh ʿAbdullāh ق said this *duʿā* is the heart of all duʿas, and anyone who recites that *duʿā* in the morning and evening will see all the difficulties in his life disappear. If you keep that *duʿā* you will live a good life, not a bad life; even with all the problems in Lebanon, we never saw a bad day. Grandshaykh ق said, "Anyone who is with me will never see a bad day," and this is true for all the mureeds. This has been passed to Mawlana Shaykh Nazim ق, but the *murīds* have to read this *duʿā* two times daily:

اللَّهُمَّ اجْعَلْ أَوَّلَ مَجْلِسِنَا هَذَا صَلَاحاً وَأَوْسَطَهُ فَلَاحاً وَآخِرَهُ نَجَاحاً.

اللَّهُمَّ اجْعَلْ أَوَّلَهُ رَحْمَةً وَأَوْسَطَهُ نِعْمَةً وَآخِرَهُ تَكْرِمَةً وَمَغْفِرَةً.

الحَمْدُ لله الَّذِي تَوَاضَعَ كُلُّ شَيْءٍ لِعَظَمَتِهِ وَذَلَّ كُلُّ شَيْءٍ لِعِزَّتِهِ وَخَضَعَ كُلُّ شَيْءٍ لِمُلْكِهِ وَاسْتَسْلَمَ كُلُّ شَيْءٍ لِقُدْرَتِهِ .

وَالحَمْدُ لله الَّذِي سَكَنَ كُلُّ شَيْءٍ لِهَيْبَتِهِ وَأَظْهَرَ كُلَّ شَيْءٍ بِحِكْمَتِهِ وَتَصَاغَرَ كُلُّ شَيْءٍ لِكِبْرِيَائِهِ.

اللَّهُمَّ أَيْقِظْنَا فِي أَحَبِّ السَاعَاتِ إِلَيْكَ يَا وَدُودُ يَا ﴿ ذُو الْعَرْشِ الْمَجِيدُ فَعَّالٌ لِّمَا يُرِيدُ هَلْ أَتَاكَ حَدِيثُ الْجُنُودِ فِرْعَوْنَ وَثَمُودَ بَلِ الَّذِينَ كَفَرُوا فِي تَكْذِيبٍ وَاللهُ مِن وَرَائِهِم مُّحِيطٌ بَلْ هُوَ قُرْآنٌ مَّجِيدٌ فِي لَوْحٍ مَّحْفُوظٍ.﴾

Allāhuma 'j'al āwwal majlisinā hadhā ṣalāḥan wa awṣaṭahu falāḥan wa ākhirahu najāḥan. Allāhuma 'j'al āwwalahu raḥmatan wa awṣaṭahu ni'matan wa ākhirahu takrīmatan wa maghfirah. Alḥamdullilāhi 'Lladhī tawaḍ'a kullu shayin li-'aẓamatihi wa dhalla kullu shayin li-'izzatihi wa khaḍ'a kullu shayin li-mulkihi w'astaslama kullu shayin li-qudratih. Alḥamdullilāhi 'Lladhī sakana kullu shayin li-haybatihi wa aẓhara kullu shayin bi-ḥikmatihi wa taṣāghara kullu shayin li-kibrīyā'ih. Allāhuma 'ayqiẓnā fī aḥabbi's-saā'ti ilayk yā

Wadūd, yā dha'l-'arshi'l-majīd fa'ālun limā yurīd. Hal atāka ḥadīthu'l-junūdi fira'wna wa thamūda bali 'Lladhīnā kafarū fī takdhībin w 'Allāhu min warā'ihim muḥīṭun bal huwa qurānun majīdun fī lawḥin maḥfūẓ.

O our Lord! Make the beginning of this gathering goodness, its middle happiness, and its end success. O our Lord! Make its beginning mercy, its middle bounty and its ending generosity and forgiveness. All praise be to Allah who humbled everything before His Greatness, made all things subservient before His Honor, brought low all things before His Kingship and made all things submit to His Power. And all praise to Allah who made all things tranquil before His Majesty, and made everything appear through His wisdom, and humbled all things before His Pride. O our Lord! Wake us in the time most beloved to Yourself, O Loving One, O *Lord of the Throne of Glory, Doer (without let) of all that He intends. as the story reached thee, of the forces Of Pharaoh and the Thamud? And yet the Unbelievers (persist) in rejecting (the Truth)! But Allah doth encompass them from behind! Nay, this is a Glorious Qur'an, (Inscribed) in a Tablet Preserved!*[35]

Additional Supplication

اللَّهُمَّ اغْفِرْ لِي ذُنُوبِي وَلِوَالِدَيَّ كَمَا رَبَّيَانِي صَغِيرًا وَ لِجَمِيعِ الْمُؤمِنِينَ وَ الْمُؤمِنَات، وَالْمُسْلِمِينَ وَ الْمُسْلِمَات، اَللأحيَاءِ مِنهُم وَ اَلأَمْوَات، وَاغْفِرْ لَنَا وَلِإِخْوَانِنَا الَّذِينَ سَبَقُونَا بِالْإِيمَانِ وَلَا تَجْعَلْ فِي قُلُوبِنَا غِلًّا لِّلَّذِينَ آمَنُوا رَبَّنَا إِنَّكَ رَؤُوفٌ رَّحِيمٌ يَا أَرحَمَ الرَّاحِمِين

[35] Sūrat al-Burūj, 85:15-22.

Allāhuma 'ghfir lī dhunūbī wa li-wālidayya kamā rabbayānī ṣaghīra wa li-jamī'i 'l-mūminīna wa 'l-mūmināti wa 'l-muslimīna wa 'l-muslimāti al-aḥyā'i minhum wa 'l-amwāt. wa 'ghfir lanā wa li-ikhwāninā 'Lladhīna sabaqūna bi 'l-īmāni wa lā taj'al fī qulūbanā ghillan li 'Lladhīna āmanū rabbanā innaka rā'ūfun raḥīmun yā arḥama 'r-rāḥimīn.

O Allah forgive me my sins and my parents' just as they raised me when I was small and to all the believers, men and women, and all the Muslims, men and women, both the living among them and the dead. And *"Forgive us, and our brethren who came before us into the Faith, and leave not, in our hearts, rancour against those who have* believed. *Our Lord! Thou art indeed Full of Kindness, Most Merciful."*[36] O Most Merciful of those who show mercy!

اللَّهُمَّ بِجَاهِ حَبِيبِكَ اَلْمُصْطَفَى وَ رَسُولِكَ اَلْمُرتَضَى، وَ بِجَاهِ أَوْلِيَآئِكَ الكِرَام وَ بِجَاهِ صَحَابَتِهِ الفِخَام، وَ بِجَاهِ سُلْطَان اَلأَوْلِيَآ سِيدِي اَلشَيخ عَبدَ اللهِ الفَائِزَ الْدَاغَسْتَانِي وَ سَيدِي الشَيخ مُحَمَّدٌ نَاظِم اَلحَقَانِي، أَنْ لَا تَدعَ فِي مَجْلِسِنَا هَذَا ذَنْباً إِلَا غفرتَهُ ،وَ لَا دَيناً إِلَا قَضَيتَهُ، وَ لَا مَرِيضاً إِلَا شَفَيتَهُ، وَ لَا حَاجَةً مِن حَوَائِجِ اَلدُنيَا وَ اَلأَخِرَةَ إِلَا قَضَيتَهَا وَ يَسَرتَهَا. اللَّهُمَّ يَسِر أُمُورَنَا وَاقْضِ دُيُونِنَا، وَ

[36] Sūrat al-Ḥashr, 59:10.

فَرِج هُمُومَنَا وَ فَرِج كُرُوبَنَا وَ ثَبِت أَقْدَامِنَا وَ انْصُرنَا على أَنْفُسِنَا وَ على اَلقَومِ الْكَافِرِين

Allāhuma bi-jāhi ḥabībika 'l-Muṣṭafā wa rasūlik al-murtaḍā wa bi-jāhi awlīyā'ik al-kirām wa bi jāhi ṣaḥābatihi 'l-fikhām wa bi-jāhi sulṭān al-awlīyā sayyīdī ash-shaykh ʿabdullāh al-fā'izi ad-dāghestānī wa sayyīdī ash-shaykh muḥammad nāẓim al-ḥaqqānī an lā tadʿa fi majlisinā hadhā dhanban illa ghafartahu wa lā daynan illa qaḍaytahu wa lā marīḍan illa shafaytahu wa lā ḥājatan min ḥawā'ij ad-dunyā wa 'l-ākhirata illa qaḍaytahā wa yassartahā. Allāhuma yassir umūranā w'aqḍi duyūninā wa farrij humūmanā wa farrij kurūbanā wa thabbit aqdāmanā w'anṣurnā ʿalā anfusinā wa ʿalā 'l-qawmi'l-kāfirīn.

O Allah for the sake of Your Beloved Chosen Prophet and your Prophet with whom You are pleased, and for the sake of Your honoured saints and for the sake of the Prophet's inestimable companions and for the sake the Sultan of Saints our master Shaykh ʿAbdullāh al-Fā'iz ad-Dāghestānī and my master Shaykh Muḥammad Nazim al-Haqqānī do not leave anyone in this gathering whose sins have not been forgiven, and no debt that has not been forgiven, and no ill one who has not been cured and no need of this life or the Hereafter except that You have judged it and made it easy. O Allah make our affairs easy, and pay off our debts and relieve our distress and allay our concerns and make steadfast our feet and give victory over ourselves and over the unbelieving enemies within.

اللَّهُمَّ اَشْفِنَا وَ اشْفِ مَرضَانَا وَ مَرَضَى اَلْمُسْلِمِين، وَ عَافِنَا وَ عَافِ
مَرضَانَا وَ مَرَضَى اَلْمُسلِمِين، وَ تَقَبل مِنّا يَا رَبنَا يَا اَللهُ وَ أَمِدنَا بِعُمْرِنَا
لِإِدْرَاك صَاحِب اَلزَمَان سَيدِنَا مُحَمَّدٌ اَلمَهْدِي عَليهِ السَلَام وَ سيدِنَا
عِيسَى عَليه السَلَام، وَ اَرزُقْنَا شَفَاعَةَ اَلنَبِي اَلْمُصْطَفَى عَلَيهِ أَفْضَل
اَلصَلَاةُ وَ السَلَام، وَ اجعَلنَا أَن نَرَاهُ فِي الدُنيا وَ فِي الأَخِرَةَ وَ اسْقِنَا
مِن حَوضِهِ شَربَةً هَنِيئَةً مَريَئةً لَا نَظْمَأْ بَعدَهَا أَبَداً

Allāhuma 'shfinā w 'ashfi marḍānā wa marḍa 'l-muslimīna wa ʿāfinā wa ʿāfi marḍānā wa marḍa 'l-muslimīna wa taqabbal minnā yā rabbanā yā Allāh wa amidanā bi-ʿumurinā li-idrāk ṣāḥib az-zamān sayyīdinā muḥammad al-mahdī ʿalayhi 's-salām wa sayyīdinnā ʿīsā ʿalayhi 's-salām w'arzuqnā shafaʿata'n-nabī al-muṣṭafā ʿalayhi afḍal aṣ-ṣalātu wa's-salām w'ajʿalnā an narāhu fi'd-dunyā wa'l-ākhirati w'asqinā min ḥawḍihi sharbatan hanīyattan marīyattan lā naẓma' bʿadahā abada.

O Allah cure us and cure our sick ones and those who are ill among the Muslims, and heal us and heal those who are ill among the Muslims, and accept from us (our worship) O our Lord, O Allah, and lengthen our lives to reach the Companion of the Era, our master Muḥammad al- Mahdī, upon him be peace, and our master Jesus, upon him the best of prayers and peace. And provide us the intercession of the Prophet al-Muṣṭafā, upon whom be the choicest blessings and peace, and let us see him in this world and in the Hereafter and let us drink from his Basin, a quenching refreshing drink after which we shall never thirst again.

اللَّهُمَّ إِنَّا نَسْأَلُكَ مِنْ خَيْرِ مَا سَأَلَكَ مِنْهُ نَبِيُّكَ مُحَمَّدٌ صَلَّى اللهُ عَلَيْهِ وَسَلَّمَ وَ نَستَعِيذُكَ مِن شَرِ مَا استَعَاذُكَ مِنهُ سَيدِنَا مُحَمَّدٌ صَلَّى اللهُ عَلَيْهِ وَسَلَّمَ وَ الحَمدُ لله رَبِ العَالَمِين

رَبنَا تَقبَل مِنَّا بِحُرمَةِ مَن أَنزَلتَ عَليهِ سِرِ سُورَةِ الفَاتِحَة

Allāhuma innā nas'aluka min khayri mā sa'alaka minhu sayyīdinā muḥammadin ﷺ wa nastʿīdhuka min sharri māstaʿādhaka minhu sayyīdinā muḥammad ﷺ w'alḥamdulillāhi rabbi'l-ʿālamīn. Rabbanā taqabbal minnā bi-ḥurmati man anzalta ʿalayhi sirr sūratu'l-fātiḥah.

O Allah verily we ask of you the best of what our master Muḥammad ﷺ has asked of You and we seek refuge in You from the evil of which our master Muḥammad ﷺ has sought refuge in You and all praise is for the Lord of the Worlds. O our Lord accept from us for the sake of the one on whom you revealed secret of the Opening Chapter of the Quran.

GLOSSARY

Adab—good manners, proper etiquette.

Adhan—the call to prayer.

Ahl al-Bayt—People of the House, that is, the family of the Holy Prophet ﷺ.

Ahl ad-dunya—people of the world, i.e., those who are attached to its life and pleasures.

Akhirah—the Hereafter, the Eternal Life.

Alhamdulillah—praise be to Allah, praise God.

Allahu akbar—God is the Most Great.

Amir (pl., 'umara)—chief, leader, head of a nation or people.

Anbiya (plural of **nabi**)—prophets.

'Aql—mind, intellect, intelligence, reason, discernment.

'Arafat—a vast plain outside Mecca where pilgrims gather for the principal rite of Hajj.

'Arif—knower; in the present context, one who has reached spiritual knowledge of his Lord.

Ar-Raheem—the Mercy-Giving, Merciful, Munificent, one of Allah's ninety-nine Holy Names

Ar-Rahman—the Most Merciful, Compassionate, Beneficent, the most often repeated of Allah's Holy Names.

Ashhadu an la ilaha illa-Llah wa ashhadu anna Muhammadu Rasul-Allah—"I bear witness that there is no deity except Allah and I bear witness that Muḥammad is Allah's messenger," the Islamic *Shahadah* or Declaration of Faith.

Astaghfirullah—I seek Allah's forgiveness.

A'udhu bil-Lahi min ash-Shaytani-r-Rajeem—I seek refuge in God from Satan the accursed.

Awlīyā (sing., **wali**)—the "friends" of Allah, Muslim saints or holy people.

Barakah—blessings.

Batil—vain or false; falsehood, deception.

Baya'—pledge; in the context of this book, the pledge of a disciple (murid) to a sheikh.

Bi-hurmati-l-Fātiḥah—for the honor or respect of Surat al-Fatehah (the opening chapter of the Qur'an).

Bismillahi-r-Rahmani-r-Raheem—"In the name of Allah, the Beneficent, the Merciful," the invocation with which all a Muslim's actions are supposed to begin.

Dhikr (zikr, zikir)—message, remembrance or reminder, used in the Qur'an to refer to the Qur'an and other revealed scriptures. Dhikr (or dhikr-Allah) also refers to remembering Allah through repetition of His Holy Names or various phrases of glorification (for the meanings of the phrases of dhikr mentioned in this book, see the footnote entries under individual phrases).

Du'a—supplication, personal prayer.

Dunya—this world and its attractions, worldly involvements.

Fard—obligatory, prescribed.

Fātiḥah—the opening surah or chapter of the Qur'an.

Grandshaykh—a wali of great stature. In this text, where spelled with a capital "G," "Grandshaykh" refers to Mawlana 'Abdullah ad-Daghestani, Shaykh Nazim's shaykh, to whom he was closely attached for forty years up to the time of Grandshaykh's death in 1973.

Hadith (pl., **ahadith**)—a report of the Holy Prophet's sayings, contained in the collections of early hadith scholars. In this text, "Hadith" has been used to refer to the entire body of his oral traditions, while "hadith" denotes an individual tradition.

Halal—lawful, permissible.

Halal—permitted, lawful according to the Islamic Shari'ah.

Haqq—truth, reality.

Haram—forbidden, unlawful.

Hasha—God forbid! Never!

Haqq—truth, reality.

Haram—prohibited, unlawful.

Hu—the divine pronoun, He.

Ibrahim–the prophet Abraham.

Imam—leader; specifically, the leader of a congregational prayer.

Iman—faith, belief.

Insha'Allah – God willing, if God wills.

'Isha – night; specifically, the night prayer.

Kufr—unbelief, denial of Allah.

La hawla wa la quwwata illa bil-Lah al-'Aliyi-l-'Azheem—"There is no might nor power except in Allah, the Most High, the All-Mighty," words that Muslims utter frequently during their daily lives , signifying total reliance upon Allah.

La ilaha illa-Llah, Muhammadu rasul-Allah—there is no deity except Allah, Muḥammad is the Messenger of Allah.

Masha'Allah—what or as Allah willed.

Masjid—literally, a place where sujud, prostration, is made, i.e., a mosque.

Mumin/muminah—male/female believers in Islam.

Murid—a disciple or follower of a shaykh.

Murshid—spiritual guide, pir.

Musa—the prophet Moses ﷺ.

Nur—light.

Qiblah—direction; specifically, the direction of Mecca.

Rak'at—a cycle or unit of the Islamic prayer (salat), which is repeated a specified number of times in each prayer.

Ramadan—the ninth month of the Islamic lunar calendar, the month of fasting.

Rasul-Allah—the Messenger of God, Muḥammad ﷺ.

Sahabah (sing., sahabi)—the Companions of the Prophet, the first Muslims.

Sajdah (pl. **sujud**)—prostration.

Salat—the prescribed Islamic prayer or worship.

Sallallahu 'alayhi was-sallam—Islamic invocation on the Prophet ﷺ, meaning, "May Allah's peace and blessings be upon him."

Ṣalawāt—invoking blessings and peace upon the Holy Prophet ﷺ.

Sayyid—leader; also, a descendant of the Holy Prophet.

Sayyīdinā—our chief, master.

Shahadah—the Islamic creed or Declaration of Faith, "Ash-shadu an la ilaha illa-Llah wa ashhadu anna Muhammu rasul Allah, I bear witness that there is no deity except Allah and I bear witness that Muḥammad is His messenger."

Shari'at/Shari'ah—the divine Law of Islam, based on the Qur'an and the Sunnah of the Prophet ﷺ.

Shirk—polytheism/idolatry, ascribing divinity or divine attributes to anything other than God.

Shaytan—Satan.

Sohbet (Arabic, **suhbah**)—a shaykh's discourse (association).

Subhanallah—glory be to Allah.

Sultan al-Awlīyā—lit., "the king of the Awlīyā,' the highest ranking saint.

Sunnah—the practice of the Holy Prophet; that is, what he did, said, recommended or approved of in his Companions. In this text, "Sunnah" is used to refer to the collective body of his actions, sayings or recommendations, while "sunnah" refers to an individual action or recommendation.

Surah—chapter of the Qur'an.

Takbir—the pronouncement of God's greatness, "Allahu akbar, God is Most Great."

Tarawih—the special nighly prayers of Ramadan.

Tariqah/tariqat—literally, way, road or path. An Islamic order or path of discipline and devotion under the guidance of a shaykh (*pir, wali*); Islamic Sufism.

Ummah—faith community, nation.

'Umrah—the minor pilgrimage to Mecca, which can be performed at any time of the year.

Wali (pl., **Awlīyā**)—a Muslim holy man or saint.

Wa min Allah at-tawfeeq—And success is only from Allah.

Wudu—the prescribed minor ablution preceding prayers and other acts of worship.

Ya Rabb—O Lord.

Zakat/zakah—the obligatgory charity of Islam, one of its five "pillars" or acts of worship.

Zakat al-Fitr—the obligatory charity of 'Eid al-Fitr, the festival marking the completion of Ramadan.

Zhulm (zulm)—injustice, oppression, tyranny, misuse, transgressing proper limits, wrong-doing.

Other Titles from the Institute for Spiritual & Cultural Advancement

Online ordering available from www.isn1.net

The Path to Spiritual Excellence

By Shaykh Muħammad Nazim Adil al-Haqqani

ISBN 1-930409-18-4, Paperback. 180 pp.

This compact volume provides practical steps to purify the heart and overcome the destructive characteristics that deprive us of peace and inner satisfaction.

In the Mystic Footsteps of Saints

By Shaykh Muħammad Nazim Adil al-Haqqani

Volume 1 - ISBN 1-930409-05-2

Volume 2 – ISBN 1-930409-09-5

Narrated in a charming, old-world storytelling style, this highly spiritual series offers several volumes of practical guidance on how to establish serenity and peace in daily life, heal emotional and spiritual scars, and discover the role we are each destined to play in the universal scheme.

Classical Islam & the Naqshbandi Sufi Tradition

By Shaykh Muhammad Hisham Kabbani

ISBN 1-930409-23-0, Hardback. 950 pp.

ISBN 1-930409-10-9, Paperback. 744 pp.

This esteemed work includes an unprecedented historical narrative of the forty saints of the renowned Naqshbandi Golden Chain, dating back to Prophet Muḥammad in the early seventh century.

Naqshbandi Awrad of Shaykh Nazim

Compiled by Shaykh Muhammad Hisham Kabbani

ISBN 1-930409-06-0, Paperback. 104 pp.

This book presents in detail, in both English, Arabic and transliteration, the daily, weekly and date-specific devotional rites of Naqshbandi practitioners, as prescribed by the world guide of the Naqshbandi-Haqqani Sufi Order, Mawlana Shaykh Muḥammad Nazim Adil al-Haqqani.

Pearls and Coral, I & II

By Shaykh Muhammad Hisham Kabbani

ISBN 1-930409-07-9, Paperback. 220 pp.

ISBN 1-930409-08-7, Paperback. 220 pp.

A series of lectures on the unique teachings of the Naqshbandi Order, originating in the Near East and

Central Asia, which has been highly influential in determining the course of human history in these regions.

The Sufi Science of Self-Realization
By Shaykh Muḥammad Hisham Kabbani
ISBN 1-930409-29-X, Paperback. 244 pp.

Through a ten-step program, the sincere seeker who follows the steps detailed in this book with devotion and discipline will be able to migrate to Perfected Character and acheive an unveiling of the six powers which lie dormant within every human heart.

Encyclopedia of Islamic Doctrine
Shaykh Muḥammad Hisham Kabbani
ISBN: 1-871031-86-9, Paperback, Vol. 1-7.

Based on the four canonical schools of thought, this book comprises a comprehensive treatise on Islamic beliefs and practice in the English language in extensive detail accompained by full scholarly evidences (*dalils*).

The Approach of Armageddon: An Islamic Perspective
by Shaykh Muḥammad Hisham Kabbani
ISBN 1-930409-20-6, Paperback 292 pp.

This book chronicles scientific breakthroughs and world events of the Last Days as foretold by Prophet Muḥammad. This book details ancient predictions of Islam regarding the appearance of the anti-Christ,

Armageddon, the leadership of believers by Mahdi ("the Savior"), the second coming of Jesus Christ, and the tribulations preceding the Day of Judgment.

Keys to the Divine Kingdom

By Shaykh Muhammad Hisham Kabbani

ISBN 1-930409-28-1, Paperback. 140 pp.

This book looks at the nature of the physical world, the laws governing the universe and from the Quranic starting point of "We created all things in pairs" and jumps into the realm of spiritual knowledge - Sufi teachings which must be "tasted" as opposed to read or spoken

---

My Little Lore of Light

By Hajjah Amina Adil

ISBN 1-930409-35-4, Paperback, 204 pp.

A children's version of Hajjah Amina Adil's four volume work, *Lore of Light*, this book relates the stories of God's prophets, from Adam to Muḥammad, upon whom be peace, drawn from traditional Ottoman sources.

Muhammad: The Messenger of Islam

By Hajjah Amina Adil

ISBN 1-930409-11-7, Paperback. 608 pp.

Since the 7th century, the sacred biography of Islam's Prophet Muḥammad has shaped the perception of the religion and its place in world history. Compiled from classical Ottoman Turkish sources and translated into English, this comprehensive biography is deeply rooted in the spiritual realities brought to mankind by the Prophet, upon whom be peace and blessings.

www.ingramcontent.com/pod-product-compliance
Lightning Source LLC
Chambersburg PA
CBHW030103100526
44591CB00008B/258